I0080899

AS IT IS IN
HEAVEN

———————— ○ ————————

HOW A CHURCH THAT RESEMBLES HEAVEN
CAN HELP HEAL OUR RACIAL DIVIDE

STUDY GUIDE

Copyright © 2022 by Kenneth J. Claytor

Published by AVAIL

All rights reserved. No portion of this book may be reproduced, stored in a retrieval system, or transmitted in any form or by any means—electronic, mechanical, photocopy, recording, scanning, or other—except for brief quotations in critical reviews or articles, without prior written permission of the author.

All Scripture quotations, unless otherwise indicated, are taken from the Holy Bible, New International Version®, NIV®. Copyright ©1973, 1978, 1984, 2011 by Biblica, Inc.™ Used by permission of Zondervan. All rights reserved worldwide. www.zondervan.com. The "NIV" and "New International Version" are trademarks registered in the United States Patent and Trademark Office by Biblica, Inc.™ | Scripture quotations marked NKJV are taken from the New King James Version®. Copyright © 1982 by Thomas Nelson. Used by permission. All rights reserved.

For foreign and subsidiary rights, contact the author.

Cover design: Sara Young
Cover photo: Andrew van Tilborgh

ISBN: 978-1-957369-68-6   1 2 3 4 5 6 7 8 9 10

Printed in the United States of America

AS IT IS IN
HEAVEN

—————— ○ ——————

HOW A CHURCH THAT RESEMBLES HEAVEN
CAN HELP HEAL OUR RACIAL DIVIDE

KEN CLAYTOR

STUDY GUIDE

AVAIL

CONTENTS

HOW TO USE THIS STUDY GUIDE

This guide was written on behalf of Kenneth J. Claytor for personal use or by use of a small group. The purpose of this guide is for individuals to dive deeper into the principles of *As It Is in Heaven*.

THE HUMAN RACE

We are never going to end racism once and for all this side of heaven because we live in a broken world with a lot of broken people. However, we can for sure give it a really good punch in the mouth!

READING TIME

As you read Introduction: "The Human Race" in *As It Is in Heaven*, reflect on the questions and scriptures.

REFLECT AND TAKE ACTION:

What do you think of when you hear the words "love, unity, and reconciliation"?

_____

_____

_____

_____

_____

_____

If you were asked about the "racial tensions" in our nation, without thinking too deeply about it, what would you say?

_____

_____

_____

_____

_____

_____

In this respect, what would your prognosis for America's future be?

_____

_____

_____

_____

_____

How would you answer the million-dollar question: "How does God view race?"

_____

_____

_____

_____

_____

In what ways is racism more of a "sin issue" than a social or cultural issue?

_____

_____

_____

_____

_____

Pastor Ken doesn't believe that you are reading *As It Is in Heaven* by accident. What circumstances have led to you read it?

_____

_____

_____

_____

_____

What will it look like when people become part of the solution instead of the problem of racism?

_____

_____

_____

_____

_____

> *Your kingdom come, your will be done,*
> *on earth as it is in heaven.*
>
> *—Matthew 6:10*

Consider the scripture and answer the following questions:

What do you think Jesus had in mind when He modeled the prayer in Matthew 6:10 over two thousand years ago?

_____

_____

_____

_____

_____

_____

In what ways *has* God's kingdom come on earth as it is in heaven?

_____

_____

_____

_____

_____

What needs to happen so God's kingdom on earth looks more like heaven?

_____

_____

_____

_____

_____

_____

SEEING COLOR FOR THE FIRST TIME

*. . . I discovered that this race issue wasn't
just something I had to sort out in my head.
I also had to resolve it in my heart.*

READING
TIME

As you read
Chapter 1:
"Seeing Color
for the First
Time" in *As It
Is in Heaven,*
reflect on the
questions and
scriptures.

REFLECT AND TAKE ACTION:

Growing up, what kind of exposure to people of different ethnicities than yours did you have?

_____

_____

_____

_____

_____

_____

_____

_____

_____

_____

From whom or where did the information you learned about other cultures come?

_____

_____

_____

_____

_____

_____

_____

_____

_____

_____

_____

What role has mainstream media played in your lifelong exposure to people of other colors?

_____

_____

_____

_____

_____

What were the circumstances around the generalizations?

_____

_____

_____

_____

What measures do you take to prevent yourself from communicating in simplified terms about people regarding aspects of themselves they cannot change (like nationality or color)?

_____

_____

_____

_____

What have you found to be the most effective strategy in influencing how other people share their sentiments in this area with you?

_____

_____

_____

_____

> *From one man he made all the nations, that they should inhabit the whole earth; and he marked out their appointed times in history and the boundaries of their lands.*
>
> *—Acts 17:26*

Consider the scripture and answer the following questions:

On which part of the earth did God place you? What has been your appointed time?

_____

_____

_____

_____

_____

As you consider how your geographical location has influenced your exposure to and/or attitudes toward people of other cultures and colors, what comfort can you take from the fact that God marked out your specific "time" and "boundary"?

_____

_____

_____

_____

_____

_____

_____

_____

_____

_____

A GLIMPSE OF HEAVEN

If the good news of the gospel is, at its core, about reconciliation between us and our Creator, then in the everyday world there may be no more powerful picture of what that can look like than when people divided by racism are reconciled.

As you read Chapter 2: "A Glimpse of Heaven" in *As It Is in Heaven*, reflect on the questions and scriptures.

REFLECT AND TAKE ACTION:

How does your experience with organized religion compare or contrast with Pastor Ken's?

- Family influences

_____

_____

_____

- Presence of a Bible in your home

_____

_____

_____

_____

- Friend/Peer influences

_____

_____

_____

_____

- Client/Colleague influences

_____

_____

_____

_____

How have people of faith affected—positively or negatively—how you view gathering in groups with other Jesus-followers?

_____

_____

_____

_____

_____

_____

_____

_____

What does an "encounter with a living God" look like to you?

_____

_____

_____

_____

_____

_____

_____

_____

What opportunities has God provided for you to experience joy, peace, and healing here on earth?

_____

_____

_____

_____

_____

_____

_____

How closely does your "church" body resemble the body of believers "from every nation, tribe, people, and language" around God's throne in Revelation 7:9?

_____

_____

_____

_____

_____

_____

_____

What strategies have you seen be effective when churches have endeavored to diversify their membership?

_____

_____

_____

_____

_____

_____

_____

_____

> *Therefore, I urge you, brothers and sisters, in view of God's mercy, to offer your bodies as a living sacrifice, holy and pleasing to God—this is your true and proper worship. Do not conform to the pattern of this world, but be transformed by the renewing of your mind. Then you will be able to test and approve what God's will is—his good, pleasing and perfect will.*
>
> *—Romans 12:1-2*

Consider the scripture and answer the following questions:

What does Paul mean when he says, "Offer up your bodies as a living sacrifice . . . this is your true and proper worship"?

_____

_____

_____

_____

_____

_____

_____

What is your biggest challenge when it comes to NOT conforming to the pattern of this world?

_____

_____

_____

_____

_____

_____

_____

_____

If you are not sure, whom can you talk to, so you can learn how to renew your mind, get rid of "stinking thinking," and be transformed in this area?

_____

_____

_____

_____

_____

_____

What does Paul say the natural consequences of renewing your mind will be?

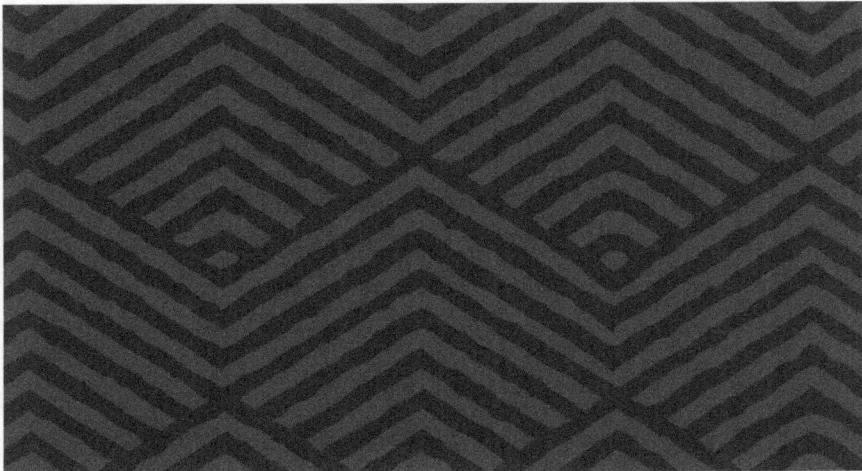

_____

_____

_____

_____

_____

_____

DIVIDED BY DIRT

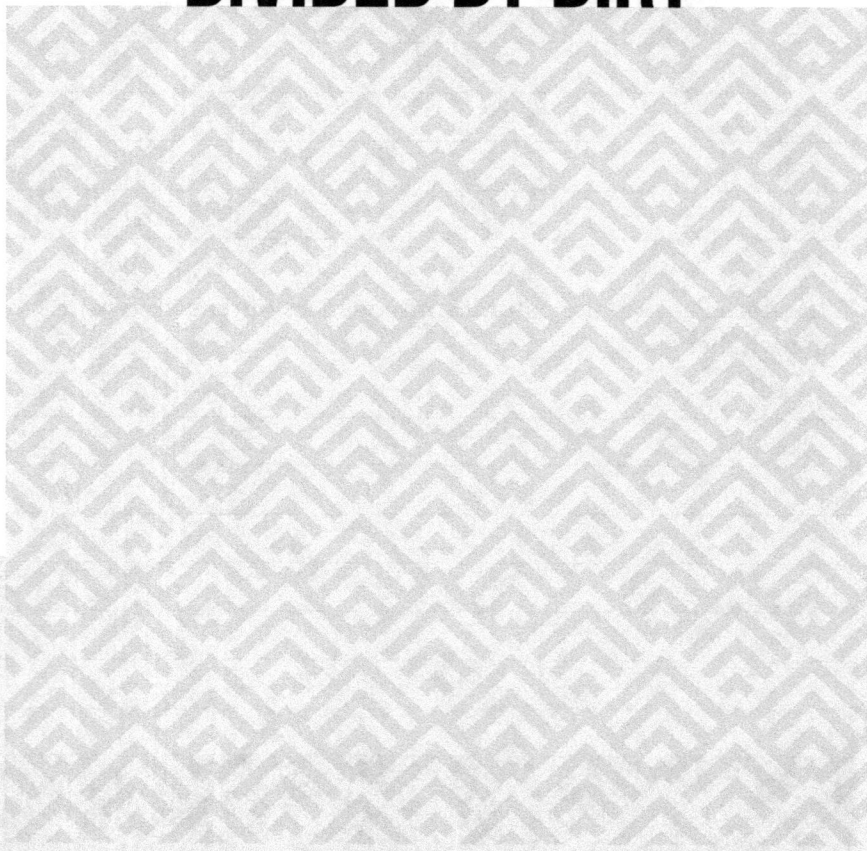

. . . There is one way in which the Bible talks about race that does divide people. It is when God speaks about His "holy race" in the Ezra passage [Ezra 9:2] referenced previously—meaning those who love Him and walk in His ways.

READING TIME

As you read Chapter 3: "Divided by Dirt" in *As It Is in Heaven*, reflect on the questions and scriptures.

REFLECT AND TAKE ACTION:

Reflect on the title of this chapter. Before you read it, what did you think it was going to be about?

_____

_____

_____

_____

_____

_____

_____

In what ways do you believe mankind was made "deliberately, uniquely, and distinctly from *everything* else"? How about individual *people* being created equally one-of-a-kind?

_____

_____

_____

_____

_____

_____

_____

_____

_____

_____

_____

_____

How does Satan use our differences to divide us?

_____

_____

_____

_____

_____

What is your understanding of the science behind skin color and other visible traits like eye and hair color?

_____

_____

_____

_____

_____

How has "race" or different skin colors been explained to you from a biblical perspective?

_____

_____

_____

_____

_____

How do you feel that various attempts to explain "race" using the Bible have helped or hindered the church's reach?

_____

_____

_____

_____

_____

What would a proper celebration of people's differences look like? Give some details.

_____

_____

_____

_____

_____

_____

Pastor Ken mentions that one of the Greek words for "salvation" is *sozo*. It means wholeness. How does experiencing Jesus' salvation make a person whole?

_____

_____

_____

_____

_____

_____

What impact could the body of Christ have on the world if those who have been "saved" by putting their faith in Jesus reflected *sozo*'s meaning: wholeness?

_____

_____

_____

_____

_____

> *For you created my inmost being; you knit me together in my mother's womb. I praise you because I am fearfully and wonderfully made; your works are wonderful, I know that full well.*
>
> —*Psalms 139:13-14*

Consider the scripture and answer the following questions:

In what contexts have you heard people quote Psalms 139:13-14?

_____

_____

_____

_____

_____

_____

_____

How likely are you to praise God because He has fearfully and wonderfully made you? When have you praised Him for making you?

_____

_____

_____

_____

_____

_____

_____

_____

What parts of God's "work" of you are wonderful? How fully do you approve them? Why?

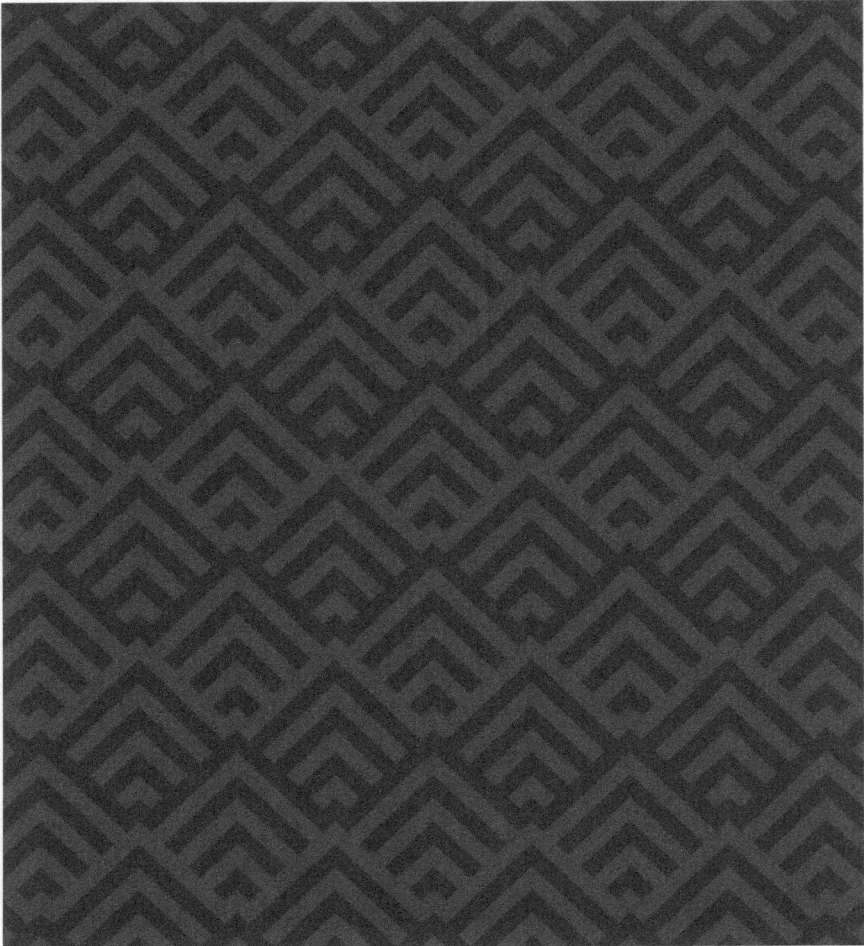

_____

_____

_____

_____

_____

_____

_____

DIGGING UP THE ROOTS

It's not just the descendants of the oppressed who have to tear down the strongholds of oppression, however. So do those who come from the line of those who were the oppressors.

READING TIME

As you read Chapter 4: "Digging Up the Roots" in *As It Is in Heaven*, reflect on the questions and scriptures.

REFLECT AND TAKE ACTION:

What are your beliefs about Satan and his activities on earth now and in the past?

_____

_____

_____

_____

_____

_____

How would you answer Pastor Ken's question: "If there is no racism in heaven, where does it come from?"

_____

_____

_____

_____

_____

_____

What role—if any—do you think the supernatural plays in the propagation of racism?

_____

_____

_____

_____

_____

_____

How have people used Darwin's writings and studies to oppress others?

_____

_____

_____

_____

_____

Which organizations are you familiar with that advocate on behalf of people oppressed because of the color of their skin?

_____

_____

_____

_____

_____

How and why are they successful—or not—in their efforts?

_____

_____

_____

_____

_____

What internal struggles do people face in their own lives as a result of racism or other forms of oppression?

_____

_____

_____

_____

How would you encourage a person who feels defeated economically, physically, emotionally, or otherwise because of that oppression?

_____

_____

_____

_____

_____

_____

_____

What role does oppression's evil twin—fear—play in keeping people captive to racism?

_____

_____

_____

_____

_____

_____

What specifically can you do to ease the burden of your brothers and sisters who are oppressed?

_____

_____

_____

_____

_____

> *For our struggle is not against flesh and blood, but against the rulers, against the authorities, against the powers of this dark world and against the spiritual forces of evil in the heavenly realms.*
>
> —*Ephesians 6:12*

Consider the scripture and answer the following questions:

Who or what does the apostle Paul believe is responsible for the evil in the world?

_____

_____

_____

_____

_____

_____

_____

_____

Why does this make the body of Christ racism's ultimate foe?

_____

_____

_____

_____

_____

_____

_____

_____

How do you suggest Jesus-followers go about fighting battles in the war against racism?

_____

_____

_____

_____

_____

_____

_____

Which strategies are you currently employing to stop it?

_____

_____

_____

_____

_____

_____

_____

THE WHO AND THE WHAT

Stereotypes are like a social heresy: there's just enough truth in there somewhere to make it seem believable if you're not discerning and aware.

READING TIME

As you read Chapter 5: "The Who and the What" in *As It Is in Heaven*, reflect on the questions and scriptures.

REFLECT AND TAKE ACTION:

What is your general "feeling" when people start talking about race?

_____

_____

_____

_____

_____

_____

What would a God-honoring discussion about racism look and sound like?

_____

_____

_____

_____

_____

_____

How do you differentiate between *who* you are and *what* you are?

_____

_____

_____

_____

_____

What ideals or ideas have helped you most firmly establish your identity?

_____

_____

_____

_____

_____

_____

_____

Where do you find or have you found your value? What about the value of others?

_____

_____

_____

_____

_____

_____

_____

With which stereotypes are you most familiar? Which have people applied to you? What has been your response?

_____

_____

_____

_____

_____

_____

_____

How do you go about breaking stereotypical thinking in yourself and others?

_____

_____

_____

_____

_____

_____

_____

_____

_____

Pastor Ken believes that some people who make generalized statements about people with skin colors that don't match theirs aren't intentionally being racist. They're just being lazy. What are your thoughts on this?

_____

_____

_____

_____

_____

_____

How do we rob people of God's grace for their lives when we don't allow them to be their individual selves but group them with other people?

_____

_____

_____

_____

_____

_____

> *From now on we regard no one from a worldly point of view. Though we once regarded Christ in this way, we do so no longer. Therefore, if anyone is in Christ, the new creation has come: The old has gone, the new is here!*
>
> *—2 Corinthians 5:16-17*

Consider the scripture and answer the following questions:

What does it mean to regard someone from a "worldly point of view"?

_____

_____

_____

_____

_____

How had the Corinthians' view of Christ changed?

_____

_____

_____

_____

_____

How will changing the way we view people change our attitudes and actions toward them?

_____

_____

_____

_____

_____

EVERY PROMISE HAS A PROCESS

I believe that prayer is an important part of seeing a vision become a reality, but it's not enough on its own. In some ways, God often wants us to be part of the answer to our own prayers.

As you read
Chapter 6:
"Every Promise
Has a Process"
in *As It Is in
Heaven*, reflect
on the questions
and scriptures.

REFLECT AND TAKE ACTION:

What vision has God given you for which
He hasn't shared with you the fine details?

_____

_____

_____

_____

_____

_____

_____

_____

_____

Where have you felt like you totally
belonged? How often has that been your
place of worship?

_____

_____

_____

_____

_____

_____

_____

_____

_____

_____

_____

How can a person know when he or she has God's favor? What does that look like?

_____

_____

_____

_____

_____

_____

When have you found yourself doing everything you could to remedy a situation, but the solution simply wouldn't be remedied? What did you finally do?

_____

_____

_____

_____

_____

_____

What was the difference between stating that Alive Church was for everyone and establishing that as its identity?

_____

_____

_____

_____

_____

_____

What have you had to be intentional about in order to see positive change?

_____

_____

_____

_____

_____

_____

What practical steps can you take in the coming weeks in order to see this positive trend continue?

_____

_____

_____

_____

_____

_____

What can a person do to make their vision "plain to see" both as a reminder to that person and other people involved?

_____

_____

_____

_____

_____

_____

> *Write the vision, and make it plain on tablets, That he may run who reads it. For the vision is yet for an appointed time; But at the end it will speak, and it will not lie. Though it tarries, wait for it; because it will surely come. It will not tarry.*
>
> *—Habakkuk 2:2-3 (NKJV)*

Consider the scripture and answer the following questions:

What do you think would be the result of not writing down your vision?

_____

_____

_____

_____

_____

_____

_____

Do you think Habakkuk was meant to accomplish this vision alone? Do you think you were meant to accomplish your vision alone?

_____

_____

_____

_____

_____

_____

_____

_____

How does writing something down and making it plain to see influence a waiting period?

_____

_____

_____

_____

_____

_____

_____

BRINGING A DREAM TO LIFE

At the end of the day, success cannot be measured in numbers alone, and church growth and the spread of the gospel are not necessarily the same thing.

READING TIME

As you read Chapter 7: "Bringing a Dream to Life" in *As It Is in Heaven*, reflect on the questions and scriptures.

REFLECT AND TAKE ACTION:

Why do you believe people think they can bring about change by doing the "same old same old"?

_____

_____

_____

_____

_____

_____

_____

_____

_____

What are the obstacles blocking you and your church from implementing the fifty-fifty rule or something similar?

_____

_____

_____

_____

_____

_____

_____

_____

_____

_____

Do you think it's ever necessary to ask individuals in leadership positions to step aside as the organization grows and evolves? Explain your answer.

_____

_____

_____

_____

_____

_____

_____

What challenges would arise in your church if you made the internal changes Alive Church made? What sacrifices would the body have to make? Consider the following areas: style of dress, style of worship, length of service, or other cultural preferences.

_____

_____

_____

_____

_____

_____

_____

_____

_____

_____

_____

_____

_____

What would it look life if you allowed others to get "into your refrigerator"? What would people see?

_____

_____

_____

_____

_____

_____

_____

Pastor Ken states: "You can learn more about someone from how they handle adversity than how they handle opportunity." When have you seen this to be true?

_____

_____

_____

_____

_____

What are you thinking and feeling right now about how Pastor Ken has gone about bringing more racial diversity to Alive Church?

_____

_____

_____

_____

_____

> *"A new command I give you: Love one another. As I have loved you, so you must love one another. By this everyone will know that you are my disciples, if you love one another."*
>
> *—John 13:34-35*

Consider the scripture and answer the following questions:

Why do you think Jesus spoke these words to His disciples just after their last supper together?

_____

_____

_____

_____

_____

_____

_____

_____

When has loving your brothers and sisters in Christ meant that you had to love them in the way Jesus loves you as opposed to the way that is most natural for you?

_____

_____

_____

_____

_____

_____

_____

_____

How does loving each other in such a way demonstrate to the world that we are Christ's disciples?

_____

_____

_____

_____

_____

_____

_____

_____

SEEING THINGS THEIR WAY

There is a time for looking back and acknowledging ways in which oppression has perpetuated inequality, if not actively supported it, and repenting of that history.

READING TIME

As you read Chapter 8: "Seeing Things Their Way" in *As It Is in Heaven*, reflect on the questions and scriptures.

REFLECT AND TAKE ACTION:

In general, what is your initial response when someone comes to talk to you about an issue that involves another person?

_____

_____

_____

_____

_____

_____

_____

_____

In what areas are you aware that you have blind spots? Who do you trust to make you aware of any blind spots you might be missing?

_____

_____

_____

_____

_____

_____

_____

_____

_____

_____

_____

_____

What is your definition of "nice racism"? Is this ever acceptable?

_____

_____

_____

_____

_____

_____

What would happen if the church took racism as seriously at it takes adultery or child abuse?

_____

_____

_____

_____

_____

_____

How do you interact with people of your own cultural group that people of another cultural group could construe as racism? Why does that seem acceptable?

_____

_____

_____

_____

_____

_____

_____

What action steps can you take involving your two buckets—one full of water, the other full of gasoline—the next time you become aware that your conversation is taking a negative turn?

_____

_____

_____

_____

_____

_____

_____

What other Bible verses can you renew your mind with, so your speech reflects what YOU think is in your heart?

_____

_____

_____

_____

_____

_____

> *"The mouth speaks what the heart is full of. A good man brings good things out of the good stored up in him, and an evil man brings evil things out of the evil stored up in him. But I tell you that everyone will have to give account on the day of judgment for every empty word they have spoken. For by your words you will be acquitted, and by your words you will be condemned."*
>
> —Matthew 12:34-37

Consider the scripture and answer the following questions:

Since people "joke" about many topics others find unacceptable or offensive, how do you understand Jesus' admonition that "The mouth speaks what the heart is full of"?

_____

_____

_____

_____

_____

_____

_____

If Jesus really meant what He said in this passage—about good and evil, giving account on the day of judgment, and being acquitted or condemned . . . would you be in good standing? Would those you associate with be in good standing?

_____

_____

_____

_____

_____

_____

What needs to happen in your heart and your speech, so God's will can be done on earth "as it is in heaven"?

_____

_____

_____

_____

_____

_____

_____

BUMPS AND BRUISES ON THE ROAD TO RACIAL RECONCILIATION

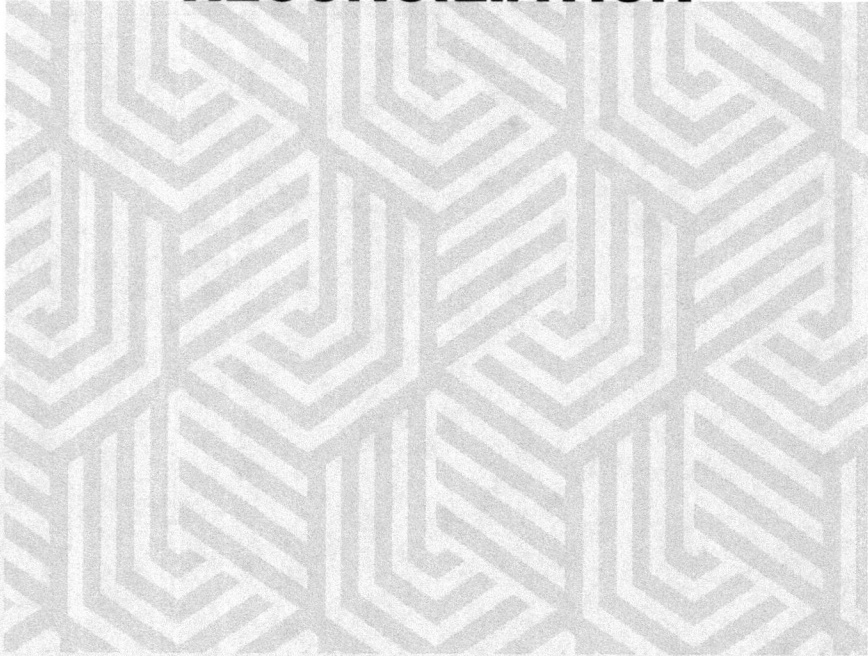

I want to be part of a church that looks a little like heaven. There's no greater vision than that.

READING TIME

As you read Chapter 9: "Bumps and Bruises on the Road to Racial Reconciliation" in *As It Is in Heaven*, reflect on the questions and scriptures.

REFLECT AND TAKE ACTION:

What is your experience with "unspoken segregation"? How did or do you respond to it?

_____

_____

_____

_____

_____

_____

_____

_____

_____

_____

_____

What phrases do you commonly hear—like "color-blind"—that need to be retired because they are not helpful?

_____

_____

_____

_____

_____

_____

_____

_____

What is your perspective of "intentional diversity"? Where have you seen it? How has it worked?

_____

_____

_____

_____

_____

_____

_____

_____

_____

_____

_____

_____

_____

How can you relate to each of the stories in this chapter?

- Melanie _____

_____

_____

_____

- Crystal _____

_____

_____

_____

- Anthony _____
  _____
  _____
  _____
  _____

- Leslie _____
  _____
  _____
  _____
  _____

- Scott _____
  _____
  _____
  _____
  _____

> *But one thing I do: Forgetting what is behind and straining toward what is ahead, I press on toward the goal to win the prize for which God has called me heavenward in Christ Jesus.*
>
> *—Philippians 3:13-14*

Consider the scripture and answer the following questions:

What might the apostle Paul have been forgetting from the part of his life that was behind him?

_____

_____

_____

_____

_____

_____

_____

_____

What tension do you feel as you attempt to forget the past and strain on toward the future?

_____

_____

_____

_____

_____

_____

_____

_____

What are you relying on—besides determination—to make the bumps and blisters worth it?

_____

_____

_____

_____

_____

_____

_____

_____

THE ACID TEST

*We know that family ties are strong. That means
we hang in there with each other. We forgive
their strange ways. We are there for them.*

READING
TIME

As you read
Chapter 10:
"The Acid Test"
in *As It Is in
Heaven*, reflect
on the questions
and scriptures.

REFLECT AND TAKE ACTION:

In what ways might prejudice "have crept into
your [or other people's] beliefs and attitudes
without you [or them] even realizing it"?

_____

_____

_____

_____

_____

_____

_____

_____

_____

_____

Reflect on Pastor Ken's "Acid Test" of racism
being interracial marriage.

_____

_____

_____

_____

_____

_____

_____

_____

_____

_____

_____

How do you see this played out where you live or in other parts of the United States?

_____

_____

_____

_____

_____

_____

_____

How does using words like "integrity" influence how people view and interpret oppressive laws and systems?

_____

_____

_____

_____

_____

_____

_____

Which sign of hope in this chapter buoys your confidence for the future?

_____

_____

_____

_____

_____

_____

Which sign of resistance causes you the most concern?

_____

_____

_____

_____

_____

_____

_____

How can properly identifying and addressing what concerns you
lead to greater hope?

_____

_____

_____

_____

_____

_____

_____

How have you previously interpreted Jesus' statements about his "family"?

_____

_____

_____

_____

_____

How do you reconcile the differences between your biological family and the other people you consider family? In what ways do each reflect heaven?

_____

_____

_____

_____

_____

_____

_____

_____

_____

_____

> *"I have told you these things, so that in me you may have peace. In this world you will have trouble. But take heart! I have overcome the world.".*
>
> *—John 16:33*

Consider the scripture and answer the following questions:

Reflect on the "life will be hard" argument according to each of the following:

- Pastor Ken _____
  _____
  _____
  _____
  _____
  _____

- John Piper _____
  _____
  _____
  _____
  _____

- Jesus_____
  _____
  _____
  _____
  _____
  _____
  _____

DOING THE HARD WORK OF FORGIVENESS

Be careful about what you consume. . . . Only watching your preferred source of news—whether that is CNN or Fox News—isn't going to help you see well.

READING TIME

As you read Chapter 11: "Doing the Hard Work of Forgiveness" in *As It Is in Heaven*, reflect on the questions and scriptures.

REFLECT AND TAKE ACTION:

In what areas has forgiveness been hardest for you?

_____

_____

_____

_____

_____

_____

_____

_____

_____

_____

What role has "the tongue" or your words played in your willingness or even ability to forgive those who have wronged you?

_____

_____

_____

_____

_____

_____

_____

_____

_____

_____

Which part of God's Word has spoken truth to you?

_____

_____

_____

_____

_____

_____

_____

How does assigning motive—or not—to the people who have hurt you influenced your thoughts about and journey toward forgiving them?

_____

_____

_____

_____

_____

_____

_____

What are your thoughts regarding compensating the living for that which was taken from their ancestors?

_____

_____

_____

_____

_____

_____

How does a person's perspective of the source of his or her "increase" influence those thoughts?

_____

_____

_____

_____

_____

_____

_____

What might you need to "let go" of, so you can start walking in God's precious and powerful promises?

_____

_____

_____

_____

_____

_____

_____

How might following Habakkuk's direction, "Write the [offense], and make it plain on tablets," allow a person to send it far, far away with a symbolic runner and start on the path toward truly living?

_____

_____

_____

_____

_____

_____

_____

_____

How about following Pastor Ken's suggestion? (You can change the wording if you belong to the "people" who need forgiveness.) "Speak it out. Open your mouth and forgive people for slavery, for discrimination, for prejudicial remarks, for passing you up for jobs, for calling you names, for rejecting you, and abandoning you."

_____

_____

_____

_____

_____

_____

_____

_____

_____

_____

_____

> *Forgive us our debts, as we also have forgiven our debtors.*
>
> —*Matthew 6:12*

Consider the scripture and answer the following questions:

Why do you think Jesus included this in His instructions to His disciples about prayer?

_____

_____

_____

_____

_____

_____

How is our forgiving others related to our debts to be forgiven?

_____

_____

_____

_____

_____

_____

What must a person do if he or she wants to be fully forgiven? How is that possible?

_____

_____

_____

_____

_____

THE POWER OF LOVE

*Remember, when God looks at us, He doesn't
see lots of different races. He sees one race—
the human race, as it is in heaven.*

READING TIME

As you read Chapter 12: "The Power of Love" in *As It Is in Heaven,* reflect on the questions and scriptures.

REFLECT AND TAKE ACTION:

What is the "simple" part of dealing with racism?

_____

_____

_____

_____

_____

_____

_____

_____

What part is not "easy"?

_____

_____

_____

_____

_____

_____

_____

How is it possible that "love" is the answer?

_____

_____

_____

_____

_____

_____

What correlation does Pastor Ken make between the current crisis of racism and the interracial couple who got engaged on a terrible day?

_____

_____

_____

_____

_____

_____

Considering the picture of redemptive love in the story of Hosea, what hope does that give you regarding God's ability to make earth "as it is in heaven"?

_____

_____

_____

_____

_____

_____

Which form of love—*eros, storge, phileo, or agape*—is our best hope for ending racism? What is your rationale?

_____

_____

_____

_____

_____

_____

How is God calling you to be part of the solution to racism?

_____

_____

_____

_____

What action steps are you prepared to take as you answer His call?

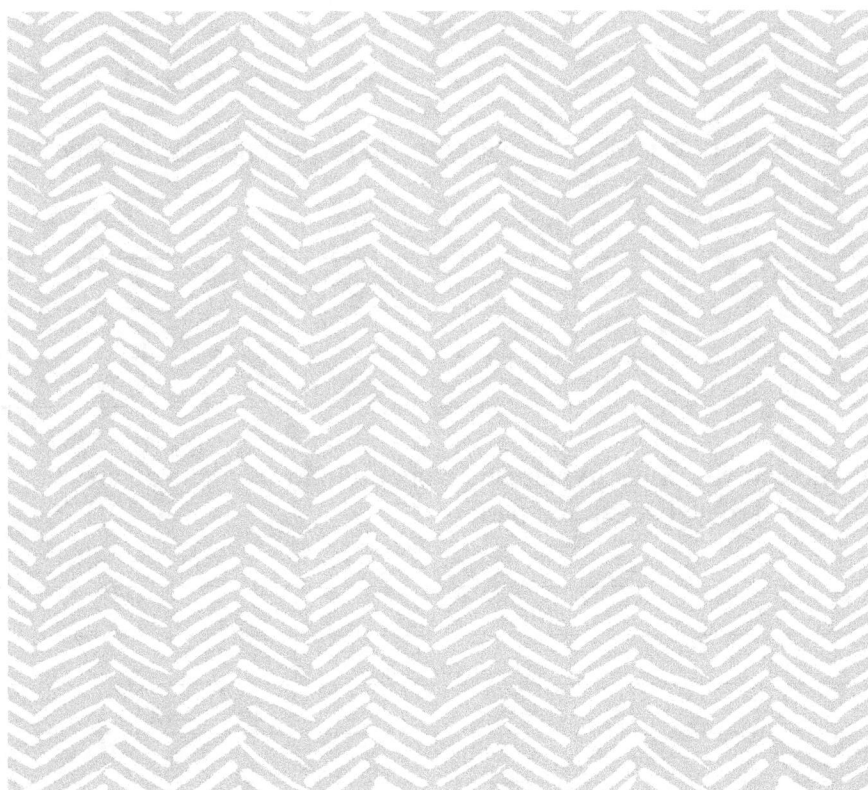

_____

_____

_____

_____

> *Love is patient, love is kind. It does not envy, it does not boast, it is not proud. It does not dishonor others, it is not self-seeking, it is not easily angered, it keeps no record of wrongs. Love does not delight in evil but rejoices with the truth. It always protects, always trusts, always hopes, always perseveres.*
>
> —*1 Corinthians 13:4-7*

Consider the scripture and answer the following questions:

If people attempted to love each other using these verses as a guide, while racism might not be totally eradicated, it would be curbed. How do you see that happening?

_____

_____

_____

_____

Which characteristic of love is going to be the biggest challenge for you? Why?

_____

_____

_____

_____

Who can you enlist to help you respond in love when you are tempted to go back to old patterns?

_____

_____

_____

_____

_____

www.ingramcontent.com/pod-product-compliance
Lightning Source LLC
LaVergne TN
LVHW052038080426
835513LV00018B/2371